BEHIND THE SCENES BIOGRAPHIES

WHAT YOU NEVER KNEW ABOUT

TAYLOR SWIFT

by Grace R. Marx

CAPSTONE PRESS

a capstone imprint

Published by Spark, an imprint of Capstone
1710 Roe Crest Drive, North Mankato, Minnesota 56003
capstonepub.com

Library of Congress Cataloging-in-Publication Data
Names: Marx, Grace R., author.
Title: What you never knew about Taylor Swift / Mandy R. Marx.
Description: North Mankato : Capstone Press, 2022. | Series: Behind the scenes biographies | Includes bibliographical references. | Audience: Ages 9-11 | Audience: Grades 4-6 | Summary: "Taylor Swift went from singing karaoke in a roadhouse as a young teen to being a musical icon by her twenties. But what is her life like when the cameras aren't flashing? High-interest details and bold photos of her high-profile life will enthrall reluctant and struggling readers, while carefully leveled text will leave them feeling confident"— Provided by publisher.
Identifiers: LCCN 2021056959 (print) | LCCN 2021056960 (ebook) | ISBN 9781666356755 (hardcover) | ISBN 9781669040194 (paperback) | ISBN 9781666356762 (pdf) | ISBN 9781666356786 (kindle edition)
Subjects: LCSH: Swift, Taylor, 1989- —Juvenile literature. | Country musicians—United States—Biography—Juvenile literature. | Singers—United States—Biography—Juvenile literature.
Classification: LCC ML3930.S989 M (print) | LCC ML3930.S989 (ebook) | DDC 782.421642092 [B]—dc23 j26
LC record available at https://lccn.loc.gov/2021056959
LC ebook record available at https://lccn.loc.gov/2021056960

Editorial Credits
Editor: Mandy Robbins; Designer: Heidi Thompson; Media Researchers: Jo Miller and Pam Mitsakos; Production Specialist: Tori Abraham

Image Credits
Alamy Images: Pictorial Press Ltd, 19; Associated Press: Patricia Schlein/STAR MAX/IPx, cover; Getty Images: Kevin Mazur/WireImage, 13; Newscom: Sasha, CelebrityHomePhotos, 21; Shutterstock: Artem Furman, 18 (left), baibaz, 7 (right), barberry, 16 (bottom), Brian Friedman, 10, 17, DFree, 7 (left), Eric Isselee, 18 (right), Ermolaev Alexander, 18 (middle), Featureflash Photo Agency, 4, 9, 25, homydesign, 8 (left), Jaguar PS, 22 (right), Kathy Hutchins, 14, 24 (right), Liam Goodner, 27, Mark Breck, 24 (left), Neirfy, 8 (right), Ovidiu Hrubaru, 26, RTimages, 9 (top), s_bukley, 22 (left), Tinseltown, 22 (middle), 28

TABLE OF CONTENTS

Words in **bold** are in the glossary.

ALL HAIL
THE QUEEN

Taylor Swift is the queen of singing and songwriting. She's the queen of nicknames too. Tay, T-Swift, T-Swizzle, and T-Sweezy are just a few. Teffy? That's what Taylor's little brother, Austin, calls her.

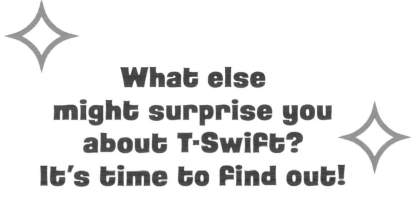

What else might surprise you about T-Swift? It's time to find out!

TAY TAY'S
FAY-FAVES

So you think you're the biggest **Swifty** there is? How many of Taylor's favorite things do you know?

1. **Favorite food?**

2. **Favorite drive-thru order?**

3. **Favorite TV show of all time?**

4. **Favorite movie?**

5. **Bonus points for the one item Taylor always has in her fridge!**

1. Chicken tenders **2.** Cheeseburger, fries, and a chocolate shake **3.** *Friends* **4.** *Love Actually* **5.** Hummus

✕ ✕ ✕ ✕ ✕ ✕ ✕ ✕ ✕ ✕ ✕ ✕ ✕ ✕ ✕ ✕

Taylor LOVES baked goods! In fact, baking is her favorite hobby. She enjoys all things pumpkin. Her top picks are pumpkin bread and pecan pumpkin cookies. Speaking of cookies, Tay also loves chocolate chunk oatmeal cookies.

TAYLOR BY THE NUMBERS!

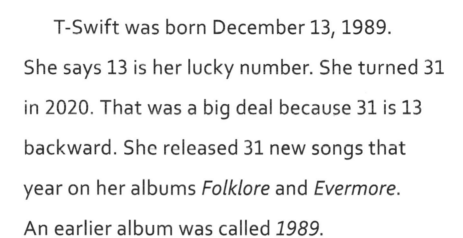

T-Swift was born December 13, 1989. She says 13 is her lucky number. She turned 31 in 2020. That was a big deal because 31 is 13 backward. She released 31 new songs that year on her albums *Folklore* and *Evermore*. An earlier album was called *1989*.

FACT

In 2021, Taylor wrote and directed a short film of her 10-minute-long version of the song "All Too Well."

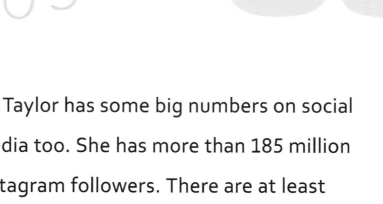

Taylor has some big numbers on social media too. She has more than 185 million Instagram followers. There are at least 89 million T-Swift fans on Twitter. How many Insta and Twitter accounts does she follow in return? That would be zero.

13

A SWIFTY
EGG HUNT

Taylor often hides secret messages in her songs and videos. These "Easter eggs" give fans something to look for and talk about.

For example, Tay is pals with actors Ryan Reynolds and Blake Lively. The couple had their third child in 2019. But they kept the baby's name a secret. That is, until Taylor's album *Folklore* came out!

◇ ◇ ◇ ◇ ◇ ◇ ◇ ◇ ◇ ◇ ◇ ◇ ◇ ◇ ◇ ◇ ◇ ◇ ◇ ◇

"I love that they [my fans] like the cryptic hint-dropping. Because as long as they like it, I'll keep doing it. It's fun."

-Taylor Swift, *Entertainment Weekly*, 2019

Taylor's song "Betty" gave away Ryan and Blake's baby's name. But fans still had to put all the clues together. In the song, Taylor used the names of the actors' other two daughters, James and Inez. Clever fans were quick to note that baby #3 was probably named Betty. Ryan and Blake trusted Tay to tell the world.

ARE YOU KITTEN ME?

Tay Tay is cray cray for her cats! Their names are Meredith, Olivia, and Benjamin. She says their cuteness is the reason for her huge Instagram following. She put them in the video for her song "ME!"

Taylor even got to BE a cat. She played a cat in the movie **musical** *Cats* in 2019.

"You can't spell 'Cats' without 'T.S.'"
-Taylor Swift

NO PLACE LIKE
HOME

Taylor has many places she calls home. She mentions some in her songs. Can you match up these locations to the right Swift songs? Some are easier than others.

1. **Taylor's childhood home in Pennsylvania**

2. **Holiday House, Rhode Island**

3. **Multiple NYC Apartments**

4. **North London Townhouse**

Taylor's Holiday House in Rhode Island

1. "Christmas Tree Farm" **2.** "The Last Great American Dynasty"

3. "Welcome to New York" **4.** "London Boy"

FACT

Taylor also owns properties in Beverly Hills, California, and Nashville, Tennessee.

TAY'S CHANGING
STYLE

T-Swift's fashion style changed along
with her music. She often wore cowboy
boots in her early years of country crooning.
Taylor also had long, naturally curly hair.
She dazzled in sparkly gowns or short dresses.

In the 2010s, Taylor's music went from country to pop. She changed her style too. First, she dropped the cowboy boots. She wore her hair straight and with bangs. In 2012, Taylor showed off her legs. She rocked short shorts.

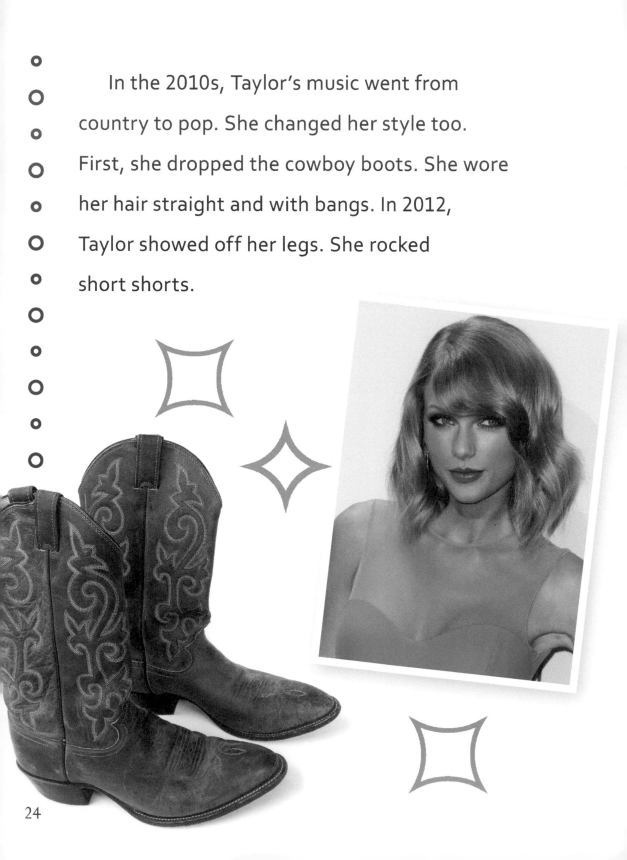

By 2014, Taylor's style was edgy! She wore hats and **bodysuits**. In 2016, Tay **dyed** her short hair bleach blonde. She even wore black lipstick.

Taylor had a softer look in 2018. She grew out her curly hair. In 2020, T-Swift was in lockdown with the rest of the world. She chose comfy sweaters and wore her natural curls.

27

BESTIES BY
HER SIDE

Taylor needs her besties. Her group of famous pals includes Selena Gomez, Gigi and Bella Hadid, and Ed Sheeran. Don't forget Abigail Anderson Lucier! She's been Taylor's best friend since high school.

FACT
Taylor wrote about her friendship with Abigail in her song "Fifteen."

Glossary

bodysuit (BAHD-ee SOOT)—a close-fitting, one-piece garment

dye (DY)—to change something's color by adding chemicals

hummus (HUHM-uhss)—a dip or sandwich spread made of chickpeas and sesame paste

musical (MYOO-zuh-kuhl)—a show with singing and dancing

Swifty (SWIFF-tee)—what a Taylor Swift fans calls him or herself

Read More

Huddleston, Emma. *Taylor Swift.* Lake Elmo, MN: Focus Readers, 2021.

Schwartz, Heather E. *Taylor Swift: Superstar Singer and Songwriter.* Minneapolis: Lerner Publications, 2019.

Whitaker, Chelsea. *Taylor Swift.* Hollywood, FL: Mason Crest, 2022.

Internet Sites

13 Things You Probably Didn't Know About Taylor Swift
insider.com/things-you-didnt-know-about-taylor-swift-fun-facts-2019-1

50 Fun Facts About Taylor Swift
thefactsite.com/taylor-swift-facts/

Take a Look at Taylor Swift's Stunning $81m Property Portfolio
loveproperty.com/gallerylist/96772/take-a-look-at-taylor-swifts-stunning-81-million-pound-property-portfolio

Index

About the Author

Grace R. Marx is an avid writer, musician, and volleyball coach. She loves nothing more than to spend her days writing, picking the banjo to a Taylor Swift tune, and walking her lovable rottweilers, Princess and Penny. If she can fit in a game of volleyball, all the better.